MW00891956

Christmas Trios

For Three Flutes

23 familiar Traditional Christmas Carols arranged especially for players of around grades 3-5 standard.

Most are in easy keys!

Soundtracks are available to download.

Amanda Oosthuizen
Jemima Oosthuizen

Wild Music Publications

www.WildMusicPublications.com

We hope you enjoy The Wild Music book of Christmas Trios for Three Flutes!

Take a look at other exciting books in the series Including: *Christmas Duets, More Christmas Duets, Intermediate Classic Duets, Christmas Crackers, Christmas Classic Duets, Intermediate Classic Duets, A Musical History - Duets, Shanties and Sea Songs - Duets, Devilish Duets, Wicked Duets, Duets for Improvers, 50+ Greatest Classics, Easy Traditional Duets, Easy Duets from Around the World,* and many more!

For digital downloads, a free soundtrack of the book and further information on other amazing books please go to: WildMusicPublications.com

Happy music-making!

The Wild Music Publications Team

To keep up to date with our new releases, why not follow us on Twitter?

@WMPublications

Contents

Jingle Bells

4

6

Good King Wenceslas

O Come All Ye Faithful

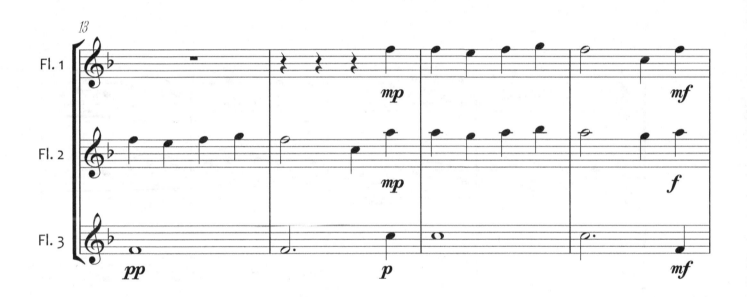

Silent Night

In the Bleak Midwinter

We Three Kings

God Rest Ye Merry Gentlemen

14

Away in a Manger

While Shepherds Watched

Hark! The Herald Angels Sing

The First Nowell

We Wish You a Merry Christmas

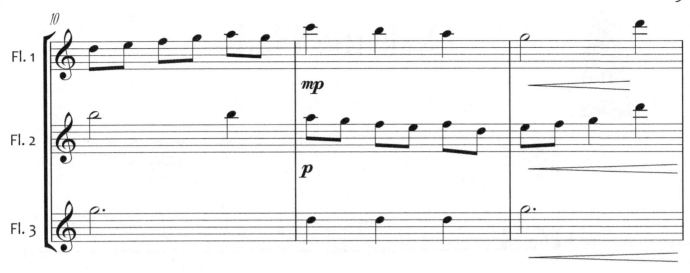

Deck the Halls

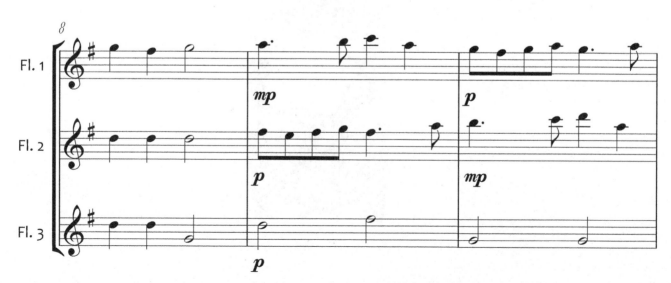

Once in Royal David's City

easier alternative flute part

Unto Us a Boy is Born

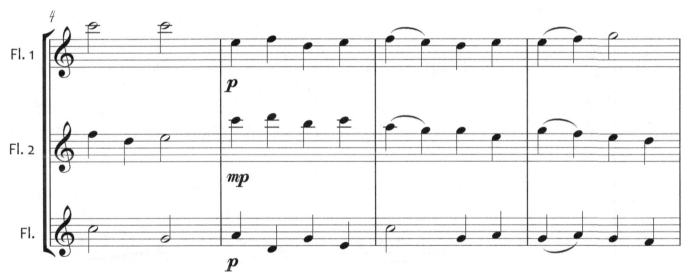

Joy to the World

Ding Dong Merrily on High

I Saw Three Ships

The Holly and the Ivy

See, Amid the Winter's Snow

Sussex Carol

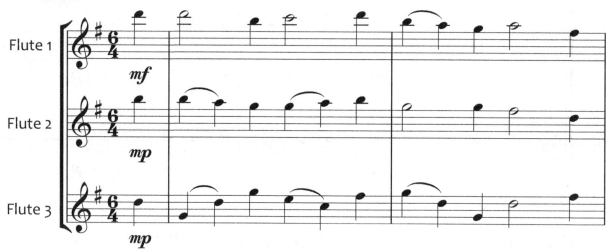

Carol of the Drum

Pat-a-Pan

Flute 1 — *mp*
Flute 2 — *p*
Flute 3 — *p*

Fl. 1 — *p*
Fl. 2 — *mp*
Fl. 3

Fl. 1 — *mp*
Fl. 2 — *p*
Fl. 3

Coventry Carol

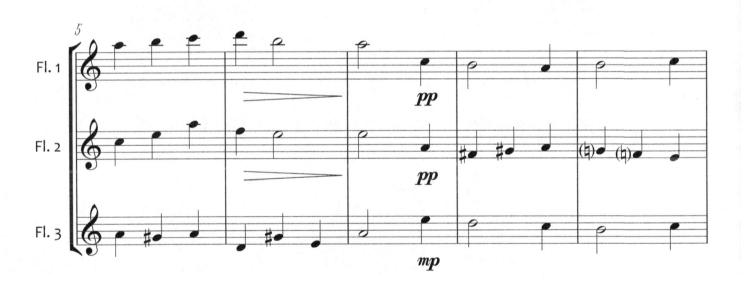

If you have enjoyed **Christmas Trios for Three Flutes,** why not try the other books in the **Flying Flute** series?

For digital downloads and further info, please visit: WildMusicPublications.com

All of our books are available to download, or you can order from Amazon.

Introducing some of our favourites:

Christmas Duets

100 Christmas and Festive Tunes from Around the World

Trick or Treat – A Halloween Suite

60 Easy Classics

Christmas Classic Duets

Christmas Bonanza

Fish 'n' Ships

Have a Banana!

Big Book of Easy Flute Tunes

www.wildmusicpublications.com

50+ Greatest Intermediate Classics

From Rags to Riches

Very Easy Christmas Duets

Christmas Crackers Duets

A Musical History Duets

Easy Classic Duets

Dazzling Diamonds

Little Gems

8 Fun Pieces for Flute Group

Christmas Flexi-Band

Music Theory

Clarinet Practice Notebook

www.wildmusicpublications.com

Made in the USA
Las Vegas, NV
23 November 2024

12488437R00026